Conversations
with
a Frog

By Karl Albrecht

Albrecht Publishing Company
Division of Karl Albrecht International
Website: KarlAlbrecht.com

About the Author:

Dr. Karl Albrecht is an executive advisor, coach, futurist, lecturer, and author of more than 20 books on professional achievement, business strategy, and organizational performance. He is listed as one of the Top 100 Thought Leaders in business on the topic of leadership.

The Mensa society presented him with its lifetime achievement award, for significant contributions by a member to the understanding of intelligence.

Originally a physicist, and having served as a military intelligence officer and business executive, he now consults, lectures, and writes about whatever he thinks would be fun.

Contact him at https://www.KarlAlbrecht.com.

Also published in audiobook format.

Of Frogs – and People . . .

This is a little book about being stuck –
and getting unstuck. Being stuck isn't
always such a bad thing, but it's not a
place where most of us would like to stay
forever.

We all get stuck at some times in our
lives. We get into situations that we don't
want, that aren't working for us. We
want something better for ourselves. But
sometimes it isn't so easy to get ourselves
out of those situations – to get unstuck.

We might feel guilty about going after
what we want. We might feel obligated to
others, or pressured by our relationships
or our sense of responsibility. Or, we may
not be sure what we really want. Maybe
it's just the inertia that goes with being
comfortable – or, at least, not too
uncomfortable.

So, we may accept the status quo, giving up a little bit of our soul each day in exchange for a little bit of comfort.

Some people, unfortunately, get stuck in really bad situations. Dependency, domination by others, psychological or physical abuse, financial hardship, or a sense of helplessness can rob them of their belief in their own value as human beings.

They become immobilized. And the longer one stays immobilized, the more one accepts and adjusts to it.

When we finally decide to break free – or break out – of a situation that's holding us back from something better, we feel a sense of power, a sense of capability, and a sense of new beginnings.

There's an old story about a frog who's sitting in a pan of water on top of a stove. According to folk wisdom (let's not try to prove this), someone can gradually turn up the flame under the pan, and the water will slowly get hotter and hotter, but the frog will never jump out of the pan until it's too late, because it never suddenly gets "too hot."

In a way, we're all like the frog in the pan at certain times in our lives, and in certain situations. We keep adjusting and adapting, never evaluating our circumstances as "bad enough" to make us jump out.

This is the way dictators and totalitarian governments control their people. They turn up the heat, little by little, taking away freedoms one small bit at a time. And people accept it because "it's not so bad – it could be worse." And it gets worse.

But we human beings don't have to be like frogs in pans. We're destined for bigger and better things. We don't have to accept being immobilized by our fears, our guilts, our obligations, our doubts, or the demands of others.

We can turn the frog factor around, and make it work for us. Each of us has an "inner frog," a part of ourselves that seeks to break free – to do more, to be more, to become more than we have been.

Actually, the frog is a universal symbol for transformation, metamorphosis, growth, and liberation. Many cultures have their stories and myths about the frog as a symbol of change. The tadpole transforms itself into a frog. The frog becomes a prince or a princess.

So, if we're going to jump out of our frog pans and go for what we want, need, and deserve in life, we first have to honor the frog within ourselves. Our inner frog has the wisdom we need to realize what our potentialities are, to set our sights on a higher level, and move and grow in the direction of our highest potential.

The frog is an amphibian, which means it lives in two worlds – the world above the surface of the water and the world below. This duality mirrors the duality of our own conscious and subconscious minds. The frog can be the go-between, making possible a creative conversation between those two levels of our minds.

Maybe you're finding yourself in a stuck situation of some kind – some situation that's not working for you. Maybe your inner frog is sending you a message about jumping out of your frog pan. Or maybe you've just been feeling that lately you've become too comfortable in your life situation – that maybe it's time for a new metamorphosis.

This book is about some conversations with a frog. Three people, each temporarily immobilized in his or her own way, seek liberation from their own troubling circumstances – their individual frog pans. Each discovers something of value as a result of the conversations, and each adopts a new way of thinking that propels them to a new place of potential.

This book is dedicated to the magical, wise, compassionate frog that lives within all of us.

— *Karl Albrecht*

Chapter One.
Frank Meets the Frog

It wasn't the end of the world, but Frank could see it from there. His business was failing, his marriage was failing, his life was failing. And, at fifty-seven, if he believed his doctor's explanation of the results of his recent physical exam, his health was in danger of failing too.

Failure. That was a word Frank had never allowed into his vocabulary – except to describe other people. But lately it had dogged his every waking hour. "Failure." "To fail." "To be a failure." He felt as if he were trying to keep two parts of himself – two Franks – from colliding. Frank the Achiever – the real Frank, and Frank the Failure – the pathetic loser he both despised and denied.

- Frank -

Walking aimlessly along the pathway that led to the tiny park across the street from the office building that housed his headquarters, he paused in front of the lone bench that looked out over the tiny pond. It was a man-made urban replica of nature, with the proper arrangement of boulders, overhanging trees, some ferns, and water trickling from a man-made fountain. The lily pads were real.

It was a pleasant place, really. Tranquil, inviting one to sit and think – maybe to meditate. With a heavy sigh that spoke of great physical tension but released very little of it, he sat down on the bench and stared into the still water of the tiny pond.

"What the hell am I gonna do?" He posed the question with a mixture of exasperation, desperation, and a faint hope that maybe an answer would come back – an answer from his own mind, maybe. Or maybe from the pond, or some magic spirit put there to rescue him from his desperation.

"What do you WANT to do, Frank?"

- Frank -

He started, hearing the soft voice with its utterly simple question, rattling around in his head. Had he said it in his mind? It didn't sound like his voice. It was both real and unreal, somehow.

He suddenly became aware of a frog sitting on a small flat rock, glistening as if it had just emerged from the water.

"Am I going crazy? Am I talking to a frog?"

The frog looked at him, as if studying him, looking into his eyes, seeing through the window of his pain.

"Now I know the stress is getting me. Maybe I need a drink."

"You don't need another drink, Frank."

"A couple of good belts and maybe you'll go away," Frank snorted.

"I'll go away if you want me to."

"No – wait. I don't know what the hell is happening here, but … I feel like – maybe I can talk to you."

He looked intently at the frog and it

- Frank -

looked at him. He waited. The frog blinked.

He sank back against the park bench, tilted his head back, closed his eyes, and let out another heavy sigh. This time he felt some of the tension leave his body. He took in a deep breath and exhaled slowly, feeling more of the tension and some of the pain drain away.

For the first time in a long time, his mind began to clear. He felt less of the sense of desperation, the heavy weight of helplessness, that had been pressing down on him every waking hour.

"What do I want to do?"

He played it back with a musing, reflective tone of voice. "Is that the question?"

"Maybe it's a good place to start."

Startled, he opened his eyes. Was the frog still there? He glanced around. It was – perched on a different rock. Was he really talking to a frog? Was he losing his mind?

At that point, the fatigue he had felt for

so long, and which he now felt fading from his body, left him in a kind of stupor – a trance-like reverie. Maybe he was talking to a frog and maybe he wasn't. He was just too tired to debate the question with himself.

He flashed back through the experiences of the past week. The arguments with his junior partners, the devastating blow of losing their biggest building maintenance contract, the meeting with the banks. He hadn't told his wife any of it – he didn't want her nagging him and telling him what he should do. He hadn't had anyone to talk to about it. He felt like a trapped animal.

"I'd like to just get the hell out. Chuck it all. Go somewhere a million miles away, and forget it all ever happened."

"What if you did?"

The question struck Frank as preposterous.

"What if I did? That would be nice, but there's no point in thinking about that. I've got to fight this battle through."

- Frank -

"What battle?"

"The battle. The whole damned battle. I've got to make this company work. I've got to do something about my partners. The employees. The clients. The banks. I might lose the company."

"What happens if you lose the company?"

"I can't think about that now. It's just not…"

Frank shook his head, an emphatic gesture of denial.

"I've never failed at anything in my life. Failure is for cowards, and I'm not a coward."

"If the business fails, have you failed?"

"Of course. It's my company. I built it up and I've been the one making it go. To let it fail would be unthinkable."

"Are you sure it won't fail no matter what you do? Could anybody else with your knowledge and experience save it?"

Frank thought for a long time. He sighed

again.

"Maybe not. We're pretty nearly out of tricks. When the big companies moved into town, they started taking all the business. It's hard to see a way out."

"How do you feel about being in this situation?"

"Stuck. Cheated. Trapped. That's basically it – trapped. I feel like I'm imprisoned. I'm stuck in a prison that I made."

"Do you think you're the only person who's in a self-made prison?"

Startled by the idea, Frank opened his eyes. Who – or what – was this frog, that seemed to be able to see so deeply into him? Did it know some primal truth? What was it trying to teach him? He might as well ask.

He looked at the frog intently. He felt an unaccustomed sense of humility.

"What are you trying to teach me?"

"Only what you already know."

"Hmm. This isn't going to be easy, is it?"

- Frank -

"How hard do you want it to be?"

"Oh, a wise guy, eh?"

"You were expecting a lecture? A slide show? An instruction book?"

He sensed that maybe he was hearing his own sardonic humor, maybe arising from somewhere in the back of his mind.

"What could I possibly learn from a frog, anyway?"

"What IS a frog?"

"A frog? What do you mean, what is a frog?"

"What do you think of when you think of a frog?"

"I think of that old story about the frog in a pan of water. They say you can put a frog in a pan of water and put it on a stove. If you keep turning up the heat little by little, he'll never jump out and he'll be cooked. So I guess the frog is a symbol – a metaphor for being immobilized, imprisoned."

He looked intently at the frog. The frog blinked at him.

- Frank -

"Well, you're not stuck in a pan of hot water on a stove. You're free. Maybe you jumped out of your frog pan."

"We all get ourselves in our own pans at times, Frank. Frogs and men."

"But sometimes you can't just jump out of the pan. It's not that easy."

"What keeps you in your pan, Frank?"

"I don't know. A lot of things, I guess."

"Name one."

"Guilt, I guess."

"Guilt about what? What would you feel guilty about if you jumped out of your pan?"

"I'd have to close the business. I'd put sixty people out of work. My partners would lose the money they put in."

"What else, Frank?"

"What else? What do you mean, what else? You mean, how would I feel?"

He looked at the frog and it looked back at him, with that ever-patient, ever-knowing expression of tranquility.

- Frank -

"Well, if I closed the business, I'd have to face the fact that I failed. I'd be a failure. When I took over the business from Dad, it was doing OK. I grew it to double its original size, and made jobs for a lot of people. It gave my wife the things she wanted, a comfortable life. Without it, what do I have to show for my life?"

Frank sat for a long time, deep in thought.

"You're a good man, Frank."

Frank snapped back to the moment.

"What? What was that?"

"You're a good man. You've done a lot of good in your life. How can you call yourself a failure?"

"Listen, frog – life is tough. It's a game you have to play. You don't make the rules and you can't get out the game. It might be another way in your frog world, but for humans it's win or lose."

"Frank, success and failure don't exist in nature – only in the human mind. Those are evaluations you attach to your experience."

- Frank -

"What do you mean?"

"If you set things up in terms of only two choices – succeeding and failing – then you deny and disrespect everything in between. With that way of thinking, if you don't succeed absolutely then you fail absolutely."

Frank found this new fragment of thought rather disconcerting. It was as if the system of rules for living he'd always carried around in his head was starting to unravel.

"Look, frog," he snorted, with a mixture of consternation and confusion, "if a business fails, it fails. You can't pretty it up. And if it fails, I've failed. My father always told me there are two kinds of people in the world – winners and losers. And he always expected me to be a winner."

"There are only winners and losers?"

"That's right. Whoever finishes in second place is just the first loser."

"That's a cliché, Frank – a slogan. Do you want to live your life according to

- *Frank* -

slogans? Does that mean that only one company in any kind of business can be a winner? All the others are losers?"

"Okay, okay. Maybe I am being a little dogmatic. Actually, I wonder if I'm being a little bit unfair with myself."

"Unfair?"

"Yeah, I mean, after all, the business did a lot of good. It delivered a valuable service, it gave people jobs, fed their families and put their kids through school. That's a lot more than nothing."

"Indeed."

"Dad would still say I'm a failure, though."

"Why would he consider you a failure?"

"He was never satisfied with anything I did."

Frank paused, tears welling up in his eyes. He felt his jaw tremble as he tried to speak. He was vaguely aware of his clenched fists, pressing down on his thighs.

- *Frank* -

"I got good grades in school, but they weren't all A's, so it wasn't good enough. I lettered in every sport I played, but somebody else was always chosen team captain, so it wasn't good enough. I got into a good college, but it wasn't the Ivy League – not good enough. Dean's list? So what?"

Frank sat, frozen, sullen, staring off into space. In a weaker, almost plaintive voice he said "He never told me I'd done well – ever. He never said he was proud of me. He never even … he never …"

"He never what?"

"… never even said he loved me. Not once that I can ever remember did he show that he cared about me as a human being, regardless of whether I succeeded or failed."

"Was your dad a person who accomplished many things in his life?"

"Well … not really. He built the business from scratch and it made him a decent living. Outside of that, I can't say he accomplished very much else. In fact, I'd

- Frank -

say his business was his only accomplishment."

"It's funny ..." Frank's voice trailed off as he reflected on his father, not as a father but as an ordinary human being – maybe the first time he'd ever thought of him that way.

"What's funny?"

"I guess I never really thought about it, but he probably felt like a failure. His whole life was the business, and he never talked about it as if it were successful. I guess he always considered himself a failure."

"And you've carried on his emotional tradition."

Frank felt his thoughts go into a spin. A dozen ideas flashed across his mind in a second. He leaned forward with his forearms propped on his thighs. He felt a rush of energy – a kind of keen alertness he hadn't felt in a long time.

"Yeah – jeez, I guess I really have. You know, I very seldom praise the people who work for me. They think of me as a perfectionist who's never satisfied. And I don't give my wife very much emotional support either. I've always expected her to be tough. I guess I'm playing out the same hand my father played."

"Do you ever hear his voice in your head, talking to you?"

"Yeah, I hear it a lot, actually. There are two things he always said. One was 'Life is hard – you gotta get what's yours, any way you can.' And the other one was 'You'll never amount to anything. You're always gonna have to fight for everything you get.' Those were his two mantras about life and about me."

"So those are the instructions – the directives – you've been carrying out all your life. One tells you to try hard, to achieve. The other tells you not to expect to succeed."

Frank became aware that the knot in his stomach was nearly gone. The tension that had kept him hunched forward, as if ready for a punch in the gut, seemed to be subsiding. He straightened his spine and allowed his shoulders to relax back into their natural position. He was aware that his muscles were less tense and his breathing was becoming freer and easier.

"This has given me a lot to think about. I still don't know exactly what I'm going to do," he mused. "But I but I sure have a new perspective on it."

He rose from the bench, looked around the tiny park, and for the first time sensed the feeling of life it was transmitting to him. He became keenly aware of the rippling water, the strength of the beautiful healthy trees, the intense green of the leaves, the bushes, the ferns. He felt alive again, alive in maybe a new and different way.

As he turned to walk back to the office, he started to say "Well, thanks, frog ..." but he was interrupted by a brief sound.

Plip!

He thought he heard the sound of a little splash, like a stone – or a frog – dropping into the water. But he saw no ripples, no disturbance on the placid surface of the pond. He turned and walked away.

- Frank -

Chapter Two.
Fran Meets the Frog

Fran parked her luxury German sedan at the curb, got out, and trudged up the grassy hill to the little park she'd always been meaning to visit. It had always seemed like such a charming little place, and many times she'd made a mental note to go there to sit and think.

And she really needed to think today. She strolled along the pathway to the little glen, pausing to enjoy the peaceful scene, tucked away in a corner of the urban office park.

The rippling water seemed to call to her. The big sheltering trees offered a cool shade, and the tiny pond with its still, clear water drew her gaze.

She sat down on the lone bench and

propped her shoulder bag on the seat beside her. She rummaged around in the bag and pulled out a sandwich and a bottle of fruit juice.

As she absent-mindedly took a bite of the sandwich, her eyes wandered around the peaceful little sanctuary. As she studied the little pond, she suddenly became aware of a frog, sitting on a flat rock along its edge. She was startled for a moment, but soon felt a curious attraction to the quiet little creature. As she studied it intently, it seemed to be studying her.

After a moment, she relaxed back against the bench, munching on he sandwich, thinking about the same dilemma she'd thought about countless other times over the last several years.

"Hello, Mr. Frog. I need somebody to talk to. Can I talk to you?"

"What would you like to talk about, Fran?"

Fran froze in surprise. Her heart skipped a beat. The frog was still there – she wasn't hallucinating its existence, but the small, soft voice she'd heard had seemed so real.

"I must be losing my mind," she muttered, under her breath. "That sounded like a real voice. Was it in my mind?"

She looked at the frog, listening intently, half expecting it to say something. The frog blinked at her.

She shook her head sharply, as if to clear her mind and get back to reality. Having finished the first half of her sandwich, she leaned back against the bench, folded her hands across her stomach, dropped her chin to her chest, and let her eyes fall shut.

"Life is a bitch," she mumbled.

"In what way?"

Again she started, opening her eyes, half-expecting the frog to repeat the question. She stared intently at the frog and it stared back. She blinked. The frog blinked.

Weary, she sagged back against the

bench, drifting into the same half-daze of despair and self-pity she'd been carrying around for longer than she could remember.

"There's no way out."

"Out of what?"

"Out of this … this … this well. I feel like I've fallen to the bottom of a well, and there's no way to climb out."

"What's the well?"

"The well? Uh … I don't know. That's just how I describe it. I'm stuck – I have no options. I've been doing what other people want me to do, for so long, I feel like there's no me any more."

"What do you WANT to do?"

"What do I want to do? I guess I don't know, really. I just want to stop feeling like a puppet with everybody else pulling the strings."

"Who's pulling your strings?"

"Who's pulling my strings? My mother, mostly. It's not her fault, really. I can't blame her for her failing health. She barely walks any more, and she's on oxygen half the time these days, Still, I wish she could be a little more considerate."

"Considerate?"

"Yeah, considerate. Actually, she's the most self-centered person I know. She's a professional martyr – always complaining, always whining, always criticizing. I think sometimes she uses her poor health to bully people."

"How does that make you feel?"

"Disappointed, I guess. She could be a lot kinder to people."

"Disappointed isn't a feeling, Fran. It's the cause of a feeling. How do you feel about the way she treats you?"

Fran's eyes snapped open. She glared at the frog, suspiciously, surprised that it was really there, but feeling it was trying to pry into her mind, where it had no right to go.

The frog gazed at her with its cute, frog expression, waiting, patiently, blinking now and then.

- Fran -

"Look, my mother is a good person – really. I love her. She was a good mother, she worked hard to feed us kids, and she gave us everything she could. It's not her fault. Nothing's her fault."

"What's not her fault, Fran?"

"Nothing, I said! She was a good mother like every other good mother. It wasn't her fault she had lousy breaks in her life. She did the best she could."

"Was it a happy family when you were a child?"

"I guess so – yeah. We had our ups and downs. We never had much money, but we got along."

Fran glanced at the frog, warily. The frog blinked.

"My father was the problem, mainly. He couldn't seem to hold a job."

"Did you love him?"

"Not really. He drank a lot. He beat us. He left when I was fifteen. My mother had to go to work to support us. She had to give up her career. And now here I am at age forty-four, taking care of her."

"You love her, don't you?"

"Uh … yeah. Yeah, I do. She did a lot for me, and I owe her a lot."

"Is owing the same as loving?"

Fran glared at the frog. "Look, I said I loved her, okay? What's done is done. The past is past."

"What's done? What's past?"

"For God's sake! Why am I sitting here arguing with a frog? Have I lost my marbles?"

She felt even more tense than before. She became aware of a knot in her stomach, and a painful tightness in the back of her neck. Her fists were clenched in her lap. Her breathing was constricted.

Fran sat for a long time in silence. Her thoughts were whirling. She felt as if she were debating with herself, witnessing a struggle between two Frans, neither one able to articulate why she was angry or what she wanted from the other.

"Anyway, she's not the only one pulling

my strings. I don't suppose I've ever really been happily married, either this time or the time before. Being a dutiful wife takes its toll, too, I guess."

"There are other people pulling your strings?"

"A lot of people, actually. The people at the church. It's like I have all these obligations, although I know I've taken them on myself. My husband wants me to entertain his business associates and their wives. I never seem to be doing anything I really want to do."

"Like what?"

"What? Oh, I don't know … writing, for example. I've always loved writing, but I can't bring myself to it with any real energy and commitment. I always seem to be keeping everybody else happy."

"Are most of the people in your life happy with you?"

"Yeah, mostly. I think that's part of my problem. I devote so much energy to pacifying people, there's none left for anything creative."

- Fran -

"Pacifying them?"

"Pacifying – yes, I guess that's it. I guess I can't bear having people be angry with me, or criticize me. In fact, it upsets me terribly when people blame me for things, even things I know I'm not guilty of."

"What does it do to you when people get angry?"

"It scares me – even when people get angry at one another, and not me. When people raise their voices, or get into loud arguments, I get terrified, like something awful's going to happen."

"What do you think might happen?"

"I don't know. They might get violent." Fran felt an old, familiar terror rising up in her, even as she spoke those words.

"When people argue or threaten one another, I feel like I used to feel when my father would beat my older brother – really brutally. I was afraid he'd kill him. And then maybe he'd kill me. I'd become paralyzed with fear, and I'd plead with him to stop."

- Fran -

Fran fell silent for a long moment. Her face froze and her body became rigid, immobile. Slowly, coldly, she said "And my mother did nothing. She'd whine at my father in a pitiful, pathetic way, and he'd tell her to mind her own business. She'd slink off to the bedroom and wait until it was over."

Tears welled up in Fran's eyes. Her chest heaved with soundless sobs as she tried to hold back her rage, which she now faced in its primal, naked form for the first time in her life.

"We were just little kids. We were defenseless. She did nothing – nothing – to help us. After the beatings, she'd put medicine on my brother's cuts and bruises and try to quiet him down. She was completely passive – helpless – herself."

"Is that why you're angry with her?"

"I guess so – partly. I'm sure she was afraid of him, too. She had nowhere else to go. She couldn't really leave him. But after he left us – I heard he drank himself to death – she met another man and he married her after a year or two. Things were better all around. We were better off financially, too, and she arranged for my brother to go to college. He eventually became a college professor."

"Did you want to go to college, too?"

"Yes, more than anything else I'd ever wanted in my life. I wanted to be a writer. I knew I could write, if only I got the chance."

"But you never got the chance?"

Fran's expression hardened, as if turned to stone.

"No," she said flatly. "I asked her over and over to let me go to college but she said we couldn't afford it. She told me that girls didn't need to go to college anyway."

She stared into the water of the tiny pond, and said nothing for a very long time.

"Do I love my mother? No. I wish I could get to the point where I just pitied her. The fact is that I despise her. She might

- Fran -

as well have abandoned us in the street – she abandoned us emotionally, which is just as bad, maybe even worse.

"And now she's dependent on you?"

"Yeah. After her second husband died, her health began to fail and she became a bitter old lady. She's incapable of showing love to anybody. I feel like I'm supposed to be giving back something I never got."

"She had a hard life, too."

"She did. She really did. Married to that drunken bastard. I know he beat her, too. She gave up on ever having a career. She was a beautiful woman, with a fine singing voice – operatic quality, really. She could have made it, big time. But now she's just a bitter …"

Fran suddenly sat straight up, as if electrified.

"Oh … my … God …"

"What do you know now, Fran?"

"I'm in the same trap she was in. The same trap. The details are different, but the trap is the same. My husband isn't violent, but I'm still a prisoner in a barren marriage. Neither of us wanted kids. I gave up the possibility of a career to take care of him, and then to take care of her, and my mission life seems to be to keep everybody from not liking me. And if I stay in this trap, I'll end up a bitter old lady just like she is."

Fran felt a surge of energy – a strange, euphoric sense of release. She still had no clue what to do with her life, but now she was open to new ways of thinking about it.

She was aware that the knot in her stomach had left. Her breathing was free and unrestricted, as it hadn't been for a long time. She felt strong.

She looked at the frog. The frog looked at her.

"I wish I could be like you, Mr. Frog. You must be happy, living in your peaceful frog world."

"What IS a frog?"

"What do you mean? A frog is a frog."

- Fran -

She reflected for a moment. It seemed like one of those trick questions, the kind of thing Zen masters ask their students to confuse them so they'll start thinking on an original level.

"Hmm ... well, in literature, a frog is often a symbol for change, for transformation. Liberation, I guess. Many cultures recognize the metamorphosis from the tadpole to the frog as a kind of metaphor for spiritual growth."

"Is the frog the last stage of growth?"

"Well, in literature we have the story of the frog being transformed into a human being, maybe a prince or a princess."

"Are you like a frog, Fran?"

"I guess I am. I made it past the tadpole stage – childhood to adulthood, but I'm still a frog. I guess all people are actually frogs, in a way. Each of us gets trapped, or stuck, at some time or other. So each of us has an inner frog, so to speak."

"Can you love your inner frog?"

"Can I love it? Do you mean ... can I not

despise myself for being immobilized? Yeah, maybe what I have to do first is to accept my inner frog. Acknowledge it – I suppose even respect it and cherish it."

Fran felt a further surge of energy. Her thoughts came to a focus, with a clarity she'd seldom experienced. It was as if all the pieces of a puzzle were tumbling into place, even though she didn't know what the final picture would look like.

"I guess that's it. That's really it, basically. As long as I'm hating myself for being a frog, I'm wasting my energies, and I can't make the transformation to the princess I'm supposed to be."

It all began to seem so simple, and so clear.

"I have to let go of the rage, and the blaming, and the … the … the martyrdom, I guess. I've been playing it from the angle of everything I *don't* want. I've got to stop taking the victim role, and work from what I want and need."

"Do you feel ready to make that change, Fran?"

- Fran -

"Yep – I think I do. I still have to fill in a lot of the squares, but I feel like I've crossed over a bridge of some kind. It's like I don't have to go back any more."

Fran drank the last of her fruit juice, tucked the remnants of her lunch into her shoulder bag, and stood up. She stretched – a long, full-bodied stretch that energized her whole body.

"Well, Mr. Frog, it's been nice talking to you."

Plip!

She heard a quick sound, like something being tossed into the water. She glanced at the pond, hoping to see the frog swimming away. But the surface of the water was as smooth as glass.

Fran looked thoughtfully at the stone where the frog had been sitting, then turned and walked back to the car.

- Fran -

Chapter Three.
Fred Meets the Frog

He was tired of being last in line. Watching other people getting what they wanted, doing what they wanted to do, going where they wanted to go. He, Fred, was fed up.

As he sat down on the little bench that overlooked the tiny pond in the tiny park he'd just discovered, Fred felt tiny, too. He always felt small – insignificant, unimportant. He knew there was another way to feel, but he didn't know how to get there.

Fred had hopes and dreams, just like everybody else. It frustrated him constantly to see other people who stood up for themselves, spoke up, and claimed what they were entitled to. Why couldn't he be like them?

- Fred -

"I'm a coward," he muttered, something he'd said to himself many times.

"Why do you call yourself a coward, Fred?"

Fred nearly fell off the bench. Had he heard a voice, or was he just hearing his own mind? It was a strange, soft, tranquil voice. He looked around quickly, to see if anyone was standing nearby. He saw no one.

As he glanced around the tiny glen, he spotted a frog, sitting on a flat rock by the edge of the pond.

He looked at the frog, half expecting it to speak again. The frog looked at him. He felt, somehow, that the frog knew who he was, knew things about him. Maybe it knew he was a fraud and a failure.

The question still echoed in his mind, waiting for an answer.

"Why do I say I'm a coward? Because that's what I am."

He looked at the frog as he spoke. The frog just sat on its little rock, studying him. "I wonder if I'm going crazy," he mused. "I spend so much time by myself, maybe I'm driving myself nuts. Now, here I am, talking to a frog."

"So . . . why do you call yourself a coward?"

"Why do I call myself a coward? Because I'm just not a fighter. Other people fight for what they want, and all I do is hang back and let them walk all over me. The aggressive guys get the girls. Women aren't attracted to the Mr. Nice Guy types. They go for the guy who grabs what he wants. Aggressive people get the best jobs. Passive wimps like me get the leftovers."

"Is life a battle, Fred?"

Fred glanced at the frog. The frog blinked. Why was he sitting here talking to a frog? How worthless did a person have to be when the only one he could talk to was a frog on a rock?

"Sure, it's a battle. It's all about power, competition. Getting ahead. That's what the whole society's about."

"And you're angry with yourself

- Fred -

because you don't like to fight?"

"I've never been a fighter. I was always pushed around when I was a kid. The bullies spotted me a mile away. My older brothers always pushed me around. They never included me in anything. The only friends I ever had were undersized losers like me."

Fred studied the frog. The frog studied him.

"Maybe I could be a frog, like you. Usually, in the storybook, the frog turns into a person. I guess in my case, turning into a frog would be a step up."

"What IS a frog?"

"What's a frog? In the storybooks? In literature? I guess a frog is a prince in disguise. It's a handsome prince who's under a spell."

"Are you like a frog, Fred? A prince in disguise?"

"Hah! Pretty well disguised, I'd say. I've never felt like the prince – always like the frog."

- Fred -

"How does a frog turn into a prince?"

Fred thought about the question for a while. He sensed the frog was leading him somewhere, trying to get him to discover something in his own mind.

"Well, in the story someone has to release him from the curse. The beautiful princess comes along and kisses him and that breaks the spell."

He glanced at the frog. The frog blinked at him. He felt an odd sense of uncertainty. Was the frog playing a game with his mind? He sensed that he was going to have to answer all the questions himself.

"If I take this frog and prince idea as an analogy, I guess I have to figure out what the spell is – who put the spell on me. Then I have to figure out how to break the spell. It's just an analogy – I don't know if it's a useful one or not."

"What's the spell?"

"The spell? The spell … What is the spell …?"

He sat for a long time, deep in thought.

- Fred -

"Let's see – in the story, the prince is paralyzed, immobilized. He got that way because a witch or somebody said a magic curse. The words, or magic signs, or whatever, imprisoned him. He's in a trance, or maybe a coma."

"What happens in your frog story? How did you fall under a spell?"

"My story? My spell? If this line of thinking makes sense, I guess the spell was some kind of message I got, probably as a little kid. I guess I bought into something – or a lot of somethings – they told me when I was a kid."

Fred gazed into the pond for a long time, the wheels in his head spinning at full speed. He felt like he was onto something – a line of thinking, maybe – but he couldn't see where it was leading.

"What would it be like if the spell was broken?"

"If the spell was broken. I'd be a free man. I'd do all the things normal people do. I'd talk to people. I'd talk to strangers. I'd make friends. I'd flirt with girls. I'd go to parties. I'd get a better job. Maybe I'd start my business, that I've been dreaming about." The energy flowed into Fred's voice, as it flowed through his body. "Everything would be different! Everything!"

He looked intently at the frog. "I think I know where you're taking me, Mr. Frog," he said with a crafty smile.

"No one is taking you anywhere, Fred."

"Okay, okay – so I have to figure out where I'm going and then go there."

Fred leaned forward, propped his forearms on his thighs, and fitted his fingertips together.

"What I got so far is … maybe I'm the one who put the spell on – in a way. Maybe all the put-downs and criticisms and the ridicule were sort of the magic words of the spell, but they had to mean something to me, or the spell wouldn't have worked."

He was breathing more deeply, sitting upright, his face animated with the excitement of this flood of new ideas.

"It's like the voodoo curse, or something like that. The witch doctor puts the hex on somebody and that person dies. They don't die from the curse – they die because they *believe* the curse will kill them. The curse, or the spell, is only a bunch of words and signs. The magic takes place in people's minds."

He slumped back against the bench, exhaling sharply. With a quizzical half-smile, he slowly shook his head from side to side, as if in disbelief."

"I'll ... be ... damned."

"What do you know now, Fred?"

"I bought it. I bought the curse – the magic. They said the mumbo-jumbo words and I turned it into the magic in my own mind. I changed myself from the prince into the frog – little by little, day by day. I haven't seen my relatives in years, but I'm still carrying their curse around."

"What's the curse?"

"The curse? What does it say? I know

exactly what it says. It says 'You're no good.' 'You're a nobody.' 'You don't count.' 'No one wants you.' 'No one loves you.' 'Nobody needs you.' 'You can't do anything.' 'You'll never amount to anything.' The message is 'You're worthless.' That's what the curse says."

Again, Fred lapsed into silence, gazing into the still water of the little pond, as if searching for an answer there.

"I guess it's what they mean when they talk about self-esteem. If you feel you're not worth as much as other people, you have low self-esteem."

"How does a person get high self-esteem?"

"How? By accomplishing a lot of things, I guess. If you're smart, and you get good grades in school, people look up to you and you can be proud of yourself. If you're good at sports, you get to be a sport star. If you're good-looking, you get the gals. Being successful gives you self-esteem, and having self-esteem makes you more successful."

- Fred -

"Does self-esteem come from the approval of other people?"

Fred stopped in his tracks, mentally. The question had thrown him out of gear.

"What are you getting at?

"Why do you think they call it SELF-esteem?"

"Because it comes from within yourself, I suppose. Self-esteem – yeah, it's obvious, but I guess I actually hadn't ever looked at it that way."

"Do you believe some human beings are worth more than other human beings?"

"Like, the Pope, or somebody famous? A president or a prime minister, or a great scientist? Well, I guess everybody is the same in the eyes of God. Some people make more of their lives than others, but I guess even the lowliest person is still a precious human being, or a precious soul, if one thinks in those terms."

"Fred, your worth as a person is not something you have to prove. It's not a conclusion you arrive at – it's an

- *Fred* -

assumption you start from."

"An assumption? You mean it's already there? You just have to know it? Yeah, I guess that's obvious, once you think about it. Self-esteem *can't* come from the outside – other people's approval of you – it *has* to come from the inside. Your approval of yourself. That's a huge idea – unconditional approval of one's self, regardless of what the rest of the world has to say. I can buy that."

"What does it mean for your life?"

"Hmm … Well, for one thing, I guess it means I won't get the things I deserve in life if I don't really believe I deserve them. Why should other people respect me if I don't respect myself? Why should they think I count for something if I don't think I count?

"How can you get what you want?

"How can I get what I want? That's a big question. I guess I have to get more involved with people. If I think I'm just as valuable a person as anybody else, then I should act like it. Talk to people.

- Fred -

Take my place at the table, so to speak."

Fred leaned forward, concentrating more closely. He rested his elbows on his knees, feeling a growing sense of determination.

"I won't meet girls if I don't go where they are. Nobody's going to offer me a good job if they don't know who I am or what I can do. I have to get out of my cave and interact with people, even if it's uncomfortable for a while. I guess that's the big lesson. It's not that I never knew it before, but it's kind of inescapable."

"What's made you uncomfortable talking to people in the past?"

"Well, I guess it was my own feeling that what I have to say isn't as smart, or isn't as important as the things other people say. But I have good ideas, too. I also have a pretty good wit. I'm handy with the occasional wisecrack. And I'm about as well informed as most other people."

"How can you become more comfortable talking to other people?"

"That's a good question – something just

occurred to me, actually. I read somewhere that the best way to get people to like you is to help them talk about themselves. You have to forget about trying to say intelligent things and just invite other people to talk about whatever they're interested in. I've thought about it now and then, but I never really did it in a conscious way."

Fred paused and stroked his chin. "Hmm …" He glanced up at the frog. The frog blinked at him.

"Actually, that's a brilliant strategy. And it's so simple. People feel good about people who make them feel good about themselves. You don't have to worship everything they say, you just have to encourage them to talk – be interested in them and their lives. If I do that, I can eventually add my own ideas to the conversation. Maybe it's not really that hard."

"What about being a fighter?"

"Being a fighter? What do you mean?" He looked at the frog, quizzically. Then it dawned on him.

- Fred -

"Oh, I get it. I started out by saying that life is a battle and that the only people who get ahead are the ones who fight for what they want. I said I wasn't a good fighter."

"Do you need to be a good fighter?"

"Actually, I guess not. I don't need to imitate aggressive people – I probably couldn't do it anyway. In fact, it seems to me that people who are extremely aggressive might actually be getting less out of life than they could. They don't attract people to them."

"What kinds of people attract others to them?"

"That's it, exactly. The people who seem to be magnetic are the ones who make people feel good about themselves. You want to be around them because they appreciate you. They respect you, they uplift you, they affirm you as a person. It's not because they're clever conversationalists."

Again Fred paused, his mind racing. He sat forward again, propping his forearms on his thighs, deep in thought. He was breathing freely and deeply.

"This is kind of weird, really. There's nothing in what I just said that I can't do. I could do every one of those things right now – five minutes from now if I were with other people. I don't see why it would be painful, or uncomfortable – at all."

He leaned back, gazing upward into the rich green foliage overhead. He felt a flow of energy in his body – an aliveness he hadn't experienced for a long time. He felt genuinely excited at the prospect of mixing with other people.

"Jeez – something just hit me, like a lightning bolt."

"What do you know now, Fred?"

"I've always thought of aggressive people as self-centered – only concerned with getting what they want. And the strange thing is, I've actually been self-centered. Extremely so. I've been locked inside my own psychological cocoon, only thinking about myself and what makes me

- Fred -

unhappy. It's as if I've been expecting everybody else to come to me, to rescue me. That's actually pretty narcissistic."

"Is there another way?"

"There sure is. It's really a matter of generosity. If I forget about my own selfish needs, and start thinking about giving to other people – helping them feel appreciated and affirmed – I'll automatically get the respect and friendly treatment that I want. I remember one of those self-help, motivational slogans – 'You get what you want by helping other people get what they want.' It may be a slogan, but it's also true."

Fred stood up. He became aware that he was really alive, and that everything around him was alive. The trees, the fragrant foliage, the shrubbery, the bright sparkling water of the pond. He felt ready for something new.

"Well, Mr. Frog ..."

Plip!

Fred heard a small sound, like the splash

of something hitting the water.

He glanced at the rock where the frog had sat. No frog. He glanced at the surface of the little pond. It was perfectly still.

With a quizzical, musing expression on his face, Fred turned and walked back into the world.

- Fred -

Chapter Four.
Frank and the Frog, Part Two

Frank had been doing some heavy-duty soul-searching the last few days. He'd thought many times about the strange conversation – or was it a conversation? – with the frog. Ideas had been spinning around in his head, and he felt he was getting closer to a solution, bit by bit. He'd felt drawn to return to the little park, a place where he seemed to be able to think more clearly.

He sat down on the small bench, overlooking the pond, unwrapped his candy bar, and took a bite. As if getting down to work, he mumbled "Let's see – where was I?"

"Where are you now, Frank?"

He started for a second, but he smiled as

he recognized the frog, sitting on a lily pad. It seemed strangely comical, this conversation with a frog, and yet he felt comfortably drawn into it.

"Where am I? Well, let's see. A lot of stuff has been coming together in my head. I still feel like I'm in the frog pan, but I'm starting to understand how I put myself there, and maybe what I have to do to jump out."

"What do you understand now?"

"Well, the main thing I realized is that life will still go on if I close the business. It won't really be the end of the world. Some people will probably be pretty mad at me, but they'll get on with their lives."

"You won't be a failure if you close the business?"

Frank chuckled. "I thought about that – a lot. Businesses close every day, and not always because the people running them are incompetent. The biggest corporation can fail and go under – a lot of them have. Lots of big companies make bad decisions and lose money – and they can

- Frank -

afford to hire the best advice on the planet. So a small business person doesn't have to feel ashamed about it. I finally faced the fact that my business isn't going to make it in its present form, but I know that I've given it my best shot."

"What about your partners?"

"Well, they're pretty disappointed. But when we went over the numbers, they finally had to understand. We had a consultant come in to help us review the whole situation. In the current market, the business just isn't viable any longer."

Frank leaned back on the bench, stretched out his legs, and folded his arms across his chest.

"Actually, they weren't as mad as I expected them to be. They knew that I'd worked long and hard on the business, and that I'd put a lot of my own money in. And, actually, when you consider the years when the company made a profit, they did OK overall. They haven't actually lost money after it's all added up. It's not a matter of financial ruin for them."

"So, what comes next?"

"What's next? Well, that's what I'm still working on. I need to figure out what's next for me, personally, if I close the business. It's something I never actually considered, since I expected the business to go on forever. I could hang on to the business a while longer. I'd feel better about pulling the plug if I had a good job to go to, or another business or something. A new mission in life, I guess."

Frank suddenly sat upright, with a look of intense concentration on his face.

"A new mission?"

"What ...?" Frank seemed confused by the question, distracted by the interruption.

"A new mission – yeah, I think that's a good way to describe it. I feel like I need a mission of some kind, something I can devote my energies to. Something really meaningful that I can find some satisfaction in."

- Frank -

"What IS your mission, Frank?"

"Well, I don't know."

"If you did know, what would it be?"

Frank chuckled. "Oh, a wise guy, eh? Just what the world needs – a smart-ass frog."

He looked at the frog intently. The frog looked at him.

"Actually, I think I do know what the mission is – or I know what it could be, anyway."

"What COULD it be?"

"Something that's a complete break-away. A new departure, a new start. I don't know exactly how to do it, but the general idea makes sense."

"What's the general idea?"

"It'll sound weird – especially doing it at my age."

"Maybe it won't."

"Well, you see, Frog — Mr. Frog? — Professor Frog? – I've felt for a long time that I landed in a spot that wasn't really

- Frank -

right for me. When I came back from Vietnam, I took over Dad's business, because he needed help and it seemed like the obvious thing to do. But my heart was never really in the business. It wasn't my own creation."

Frank reached down, plucked a long blade of grass from between the paving stones, and began to toy with it, as he collected the bits and pieces of the story.

"And, I got married because that seemed like the obvious thing to do, too. But the truth is, it was never an exciting relationship, for either of us. And we've grown further and further apart over the years. She's still fairly young, and I know she wants something else out of life. In fact, we talked about it this week, for the first time ever. I don't think she actually wants to stay married either – not really."

"And the mission?"

"The mission? Oh, yeah. Well, after I realized that my partners wouldn't hang me, and my wife probably wanted to go her own way, I started thinking about

- Frank -

something I hadn't thought about for a long time. And now, it actually seems like it could be possible."

Frank leaned forward, propped his elbows on his knees, and cupped his chin in his hands.

"When I was in Vietnam, I had an experience – a positive one, actually – that left a permanent mark on me. We were wrapping up an area in the highlands, driving the VC out and 'pacifying' the region, as the top brass called it. There had been a lot of destruction. Things had finally quieted down, but we were ordered to stick around for a few days to make sure everything was stabilized."

Frank gazed into the pond, seeing the images in his mind, feeling transported back to an earlier time.

"The people in the village were trying to rebuild what they could. Some of the huts had burned down, their bridge was destroyed, and their crude water distribution system was pretty well trashed. I asked the guys in my squad if

- Frank -

they'd be willing to help the people repair things. They all agreed, and we went at it. It was surprising how much we got done in a few days. We rebuilt their bridge, and we got the water system working again. And we rebuilt most of the huts."

Frank smiled, a wistful, faraway smile.

"They hadn't been particularly friendly to us – mostly scared of us, I'm sure. But after the VC had come through, destroying everything they could, and they saw us helping them rebuild it, I guess they appreciated it."

"You must have felt very good about what you'd done."

"Yeah. When we left, everybody in the village came out to see us off. The elders gave us some little gifts, and the little kids all sang us a song – I don't know what it meant."

Frank felt the tears welling up in his eyes, rolling down his cheeks. He wiped away the tears with the back of his hand.

"After all these years, I can still see the

- Frank -

looks on their faces – the gratitude, the simple innocence, the vulnerability. They were just poor, hard-working people, caught in the crossfire. Their only crime was being in the wrong place at the wrong time, and I felt so sorry for them. The other guys and I were just happy that we could do something for them. We'd spent so much of our energy destroying things, and it felt so different to be actually building things up."

The tears came again, and Frank's chest heaved with the silent sobs. He sniffled, and wiped away the tears again.

"That was probably the most positive experience I ever had while I was in the combat zone – maybe even one of the most gratifying experiences of my life. I'll never forget those faces ..."

"Is that part of the mission you're thinking about?"

"Yeah. I guess, in a way, I've always thought of business as a kind of warfare. You spend a lot of time thinking about how to defeat your competitors – they're the enemy. I think I'm at a point in my

- *Frank* -

life where I'd like to stop fighting. I'd like to spend less time getting, and more time giving."

"How could you do that?"

"Well, I've got some ideas, actually. It sounds pretty far out, but ..."

"What's so far out about it?"

"Well, it would be so out of character for me. A lot of people would probably be surprised if I did what I'm thinking of. Some of them would probably laugh."

"Is that a reason not to do it?"

"Not necessarily. If I go by how I really feel about it – what I really want – they'll just have to like it or lump it."

"So, what are you thinking of doing?"

"I want to do something that's socially useful. Something like that little episode during the war. I'd like to join the Peace Corps, or get a job with the International Red Cross, or go to work for one of the peacekeeping agencies. There are so many people, in so many countries, whose lives have been torn up by war,

- Frank -

and violence, and just poverty. I look down at this belly hanging over my belt, and I realize how lucky I really am. I've been complaining about my problems but, my God – those people in Vietnam would love to have the problems I have. They'd trade places with me in a heartbeat."

"What's standing in the way of your new mission, Frank?"

"What's standing in the way? Well ... not much, actually. I mean, nothing that I can't deal with."

He sat for a moment, gazing into the pond, running through his mental checklist.

Frank looked at the frog, intently, a little smile creeping across his face. The frog blinked at him.

"I guess, Mr. Frog," he said, standing up – feeling taller, stronger, and freer than he'd felt in a long time – "I guess I'm about ready to jump out of my frog pan. See you later."

- Frank -

He turned to leave, looking back over his shoulder.

Plip!

Chapter Five.
Fran and the Frog, Part Two

Life had felt like one big wrestling match for Fran, over the last week or so – an emotional wrestling match. She knew she had to get out of her situation. And she felt sure she could do it, somehow. But she still felt tied down, anchored to the situation.

She took a sip from her water bottle as she sat down on the familiar little bench that overlooked the pond. She felt strangely unsettled – energized, yet apprehensive. Maybe even fearful.

She sat back, sighed, and closed her eyes. "Mr. Frog? Are you there? It's Fran. I think I need another frog-therapy session."

She opened her eyes lazily and glanced

- Fran -

around the little park – the rocks, the lily pad, the clear, still water – almost expecting to catch a glimpse of her amphibian therapist. She felt disappointed, even sad, at not seeing the frog.

"Well, maybe that was all an hallucination. I guess there really wasn't a frog. It all seemed so real, though …"

She closed her eyes again and drifted off into a dreamy, half-conscious reverie. She took in a deep breath and released a heavy sigh.

"It's harder than I thought it would be," she mused.

"What's harder, Fran?"

Fran started, her eyes snapped open, and she was elated to see her little friend perched on the familiar flat rock beside the little pond.

"Well, there you are! I thought you'd abandoned me."

The frog blinked, gazing at her with its patient, all-knowing expression.

- Fran -

"What's harder?"

Fran felt a renewed sense of confidence and strength as she sat back and closed her eyes again. Weird as it seemed, having the frog to talk to gave her a feeling of courage and confidence – which she heartily welcomed.

"What's harder? Making the jump from frog to princess. Getting out of my situation. Cutting the puppet-strings – whatever you want to call it."

"What's the hardest part?"

"The hardest part? That's easy – it's dealing with the guilt. I always knew it would be hard, but jeez, it's got me by the throat."

"When do you feel guilty?"

"I feel guilty whenever I think about making the break – actually getting out of the situation. I get scared. Leaving my husband, putting my mother into an elder-care home, cutting the other ties, trying to build a career."

"What does the guilt feel like?"

- Fran -

"What does it feel like? What do you mean 'what does it feel like?' It feels like guilt. Guilt is guilt."

Fran stared at the frog, a puzzled look on her face. She knew the frog was inviting her to think deeper, to go to the source of the guilt.

"What does the guilt feel like? It feels like a threat. It seems like something bad will happen to me – something really terrible – if I don't back off from what I want to do."

"Does the guilt have a picture? A face? If it were a physical thing, what would it look like?"

"That's a weird question. Hmm ... I'm looking for a picture, an image that fits ... Yes, there is a picture, actually. I visualize it as an axe hanging over my head. If I do anything they don't want me to do, the axe will fall on me."

"Who are THEY?"

"They? Who are they? Uh ... I guess it's all the people pulling my strings. My mother, and my husband, and all the other people I feel obligated to. All those people in my life I've been trying to keep happy."

"Why do you have to keep THEM happy? Do they have to keep YOU happy?"

"Huh … Two very good questions. No, they don't have to keep me happy. And if that's true, then why do I feel I have to keep them happy?"

"What happens if you don't keep them happy?

Fran sat upright. Her head snapped up, as she caught a flash of insight. She looked at the frog, intently. The frog looked at her, perhaps expectantly.

"Wait a second – maybe I'm not thinking of it the right way. Maybe what I've been trying to do all my life has not been to make people happy. Maybe what I've been trying to do is to keep them from being *unhappy* – or mad – with me."

She paused, letting these new insights settle into place, linking up with the other pieces of the puzzle. The picture was getting clearer, step by step.

"I realized I can't stand it when people raise their voices, or shout, or argue or criticize. I run around trying to pacify everybody, trying to keep them from getting angry."

"Where did that habit come from, Fran?"

"Now I realize where it came from. It came from when I was a little girl, and I couldn't bear the fighting. The violence, the threats of violence, the conflict, the tension. I became the peacemaker, the pacifier, the pleaser."

She paused, as if re-running an old experience in her mind.

"But it wasn't for their benefit, really. It was for mine. I grew up with a phobia about other people's anger, and about criticism and disapproval. I couldn't bear to have anybody criticize me or find fault with me. I couldn't bear to have other people blame me for things."

Fran sat forward, a look of intense concentration on her face. She saw a flurry of images, memories from her growing-up years, flashing by.

"It was all part of the fear of conflict. If someone blamed me for something, no matter how unjust the accusation, I'd go to neurotic lengths to defend myself. I'd try to talk them out of the criticism, or I'd try to explain myself or defend myself to the other people who might be involved."

"What about the guilt?"

"Well, now I'm beginning to think of it differently. I don't think it's really guilt I'm feeling about jumping out of my situation. It's fear – a strange, irrational fear that they'll be angry with me. They'll disapprove of me, they'll criticize me."

She chuckled. "Actually, it's the fear that they won't love me. That they'll reject me. Maybe my inner child – or my inner frog – thinks they'll kill me."

"How can you deal with that fear?"

"It's just dawning on me, this very moment. The realization is hitting me like a ton of bricks. If they don't want to love me, they won't – whether I try to pacify them and make them happy or not. If they do want to love me, then I shouldn't have to earn their love anyway. The simple fact is, they'll love me or they won't, and there's no point in trying to bribe them into respecting me. It doesn't work, anyway."

"You're a good person, Fran."

"What ...? I'm ... well, I guess so, yeah."

"You've done a lot of good for other people."

"Yeah – I guess I have. Sure."

"Do you deserve to be happy?"

"Do I deserve to be happy? Well, yeah, the answer's obvious. Everybody deserves to be happy. But the question sounds kind of funny when it applies to me. I guess I've got a kind of double standard – one way for other people and another way for me. I can say somebody else deserves to be happy, but when I say I deserve to be happy it sounds strange."

"Try saying it a few times."

"I deserve be happy. I deserve to be

happy." It felt funny to be toying with such a simple sentence – such a simple idea.

"I can say it in different ways. I deserve to be *happy*. I *deserve* to be happy. *I* deserve to be happy."

She smiled to herself, tossing a sidelong glance at the frog.

"The more I say it, the more normal it sounds. It sounds right – so simple."

"If you say it many times, will you believe it more and more?"

"Yes – I'm sure I will. A simple statement like that has real power. *I deserve to be happy.* I'm going to say it at least 100 times a day."

"How do you feel when you say it?"

"How do I feel? I feel … justified. Vindicated. I feel like what I want to do is legitimate. If I have a right to be happy, that means I have the right to do the things that will make me happy, so long as I don't hurt anybody else."

"As you pay attention to the feeling,

Fran, can you let it get stronger? Can you hold on to it?"

"Let me see – I deserve to be happy. That feeling of being strong, and confident in myself – yes, I can hold on to it."

"Now can you hold on to that feeling as you think about telling the others what you plan to do?"

"Oh, boy – let me see … Okay, I can see my mother. I'm telling her I intend to make a career for myself. I'm holding on to the strong feeling. Jeez – this feels strange. The two feelings are mixed. I feel half-afraid and half-confident. The two feelings are competing in my mind."

"Can you see the scene again, and this time can you make the positive feeling stronger?"

"Yeah – it's getting stronger. I feel like I can explain things to her without caving in, and without becoming sullen or defensive. It's like the confident feeling is beginning to override the scared feeling. Boy, this is weird!"

"Actually, it's normal. It's the way

your mind works."

"That was really strange, though. I'll bet if I do that little mental rehearsal a lot of times, I can get to the point where I can tell her how I feel about my life, and what I want to do. Maybe she'll even accept it, but if she doesn't …"

"If she doesn't?"

"If she doesn't, I'll still go ahead with my plan, and I'll try to handle the situation with her as kindly and lovingly as I can."

"And your husband?"

"Yeah – I guess I need to rehearse something for him, too. It's not like the situation with my mother – she's an invalid and he's not. Still, he's been having a lot of problems of his own, and I've been feeling guilty about letting him down. He needs me, too, just in a different way."

"Do you like movies, Fran?"

"Movies? Do I like movies? Yeah – I go to the movies fairly often. What …? Why would you ask me that?"

- Fran -

"Have you ever thought that life is like a movie?"

"Life is like a movie. Let me think about that. I have no idea where you're taking me – I know, I know, just inside my own mind."

She sat back on the bench, twirling her hair, pondering this new and peculiar proposition.

"Well, I guess we go along recording everything we experience, sort of like making a movie. And we can replay our movies – our experiences – when we want to."

She chuckled. "And even when we don't want to."

Fran found this idea of mental movies rather intriguing. Maybe there was something here she could use.

"Also, I guess, our brains really do work a little bit like movie cameras, or video cameras. There's a picture track and a sound track. When I remember some experience from the past, I can see the pictures and also hear the sounds – to some extent, anyway."

"Do you have feelings when you're replaying your movies?"

"Feelings? Oh, yeah – the feeling comes along with the picture and sound."

She glanced at the frog. The frog blinked at her.

"So, you're saying there's a third track – the feeling track. It's a three-track movie, not two."

"You're saying it."

She chuckled. "Okay, okay – it's my job to get clear on this."

"Is your life a movie, Fran?"

"Is my life a movie …? Yes, of course. Everybody's life is a movie, once you think about it that way."

She sat upright, a quizzical expression on her face.

"I have a movie in my head that's been my life up to this moment. But what about the rest of the movie? What's it going to be?"

- Fran -

"Maybe it will be whatever you want it to be - or whatever you allow it to be."

"You mean I'm the one who's making the movie? Now, that's a wild thought. Can I decide what the movie is, and then decide to live my movie?"

Fran became aware that her heart was racing. She was sitting straight up, as if ready for action. The excitement of this new possibility raced through her body.

"So ... I guess the big question is – if my life is a movie, then am I the producer and the director of the movie?" She chuckled. "Or ... or – am I just the one working the camera?"

"What would be the difference?"

"Well, if I'm just the camera operator, then I'm letting the movie turn out however it's going to turn out. It's everybody else's movie – not mine. But if I'm the producer and director, then I decide what the movie is – how I want it to turn out."

She clapped her hands together,

- Fran -

enthusiastically.

"That's it! I have to make my own movie. If I know what movie I'm producing, then I'm more likely to act my part in a way that helps the movie come true. I can't guarantee that everything will happen according to my script, but it puts the odds in my favor. I'm programming my brain for success."

"And you tend to get what you program for."

"Right – I tend to get what I program for. That's absolutely true."

Fran stood up, feeling taller, and stronger, and more sure of herself than she'd ever felt in her life. She tucked her water bottle into her shoulder bag, slung the bag across her shoulder, and walked toward the entrance to the little park.

She smiled, and turned –

Plip!

- Fran -

Chapter Six.
Fred and the Frog, Part Two

"Now I'm more confused than ever," Fred grumbled, as he slumped down on the bench. He sat back, sighed, and gazed up into the trees.

"Confused about what, Fred?"

Fred started, looking around. Was it the frog? His gaze darted around the little park. There it was. His frog-guru, sitting quietly on the lily pad.

"Hi, boss," he said, a bit flippantly but with a note of respect in his voice. "What's new?"

"What's new with you?"

"Me? What's new with me? Maybe a lot, maybe nothing. I feel like things have changed, but I'm still stuck. Now I don't know *what's* going on in my life."

- Fred -

"You're still stuck?"

"Yeah. I was all revved up after the last conversation – or therapy session? It felt like I was getting somewhere. Actually, I did make some pretty good progress. I've been coming out of my shell a lot more, and interacting with people. So that part's good."

"And the other part?"

"The other part is I don't know what to do with my life. I feel like I'm wandering around in circles, with no direction. My job isn't all that secure, and I don't really have a profession, as such. I should have finished college, I guess, but I needed to get a job to support myself. I guess I could just get some other job, but what would be the point? That's not really going anywhere."

"Where do you want to go?"

Fred sighed, looking intently at the frog. He shook his head, slowly. The frog looked intently at Fred.

"You sure know how to ask the tough questions. Where do I want to go? What do I want to do? I honestly don't know."

"If you did know, what would the answer be?"

"What …?" Fred grinned, sheepishly. "For a second, there, I thought I was going to answer your question. That's a good trick."

He studied the frog. The frog studied him.

"Well, there are some things I'm good at. I've been trying to take stock of my strengths, like the career counselors tell you to do. But I can't really narrow it down. I feel like I'm reluctant to commit to one thing, in case it's the wrong thing. It's like I have to give up the chance to do everything else if I choose some one thing."

"So you're choosing nothing?"

"No – I'm not choosing …"

Fred stopped in his tracks. The idea had suddenly turned his thinking process upside down. Not choosing was the same as choosing nothing?

- Fred -

"Wait a sec – you're right, actually." He chuckled. "Naturally, you're right – you're The Frog. If I don't choose something, then I'm actually choosing nothing. Jeez – I hadn't thought about it that way. So, if I choose something, or I choose nothing, I'm making a choice either way."

"Not to decide is to decide, Fred."

"Yeah – I dig it. If I fail to make a choice for what I want to do, then the default choice gets handed to me. So, I suppose, in a way, I chose the default option."

"What's the default option?"

"In my case, the default option is to continue to drift. I take whatever other people hand me – there's that passive attitude again. If I lose my job, I take some other job, whatever I can get. If I don't take the initiative with girls, I get nobody, or I tie up with whoever happens along. I'm not creating anything of my own. I'm always accepting whatever the world chooses to offer me."

Fred sat for a long time, gazing into the

- Fred -

little pond, absent-mindedly studying the rocks and the tiny fish he could see below the clear surface. His mind was piecing together the puzzle of options, actions, and results.

"It seems to me that the inability to choose is not actually a logical problem – not really a matter of the choices and the pros and cons. Seems like it's really a psychological issue, or an emotional issue. There are a lot of good choices, actually. And if I'm willing to work hard, I can probably make a lot of them successful.

I think maybe people who are like me get stuck because they're *afraid* to choose, not because they don't have good choices or because they don't know how to choose."

"What makes you afraid to choose?"

"Fear of failing, I guess. Yeah – I suppose that's it. It's easy to stay stuck in my situation because it's not intolerable. I can live with it. And every time I think about jumping out of my trap and doing something else, I get a panicky feeling.

- Fred -

Maybe I'll fail."

"What happens if you fail?"

"If I fail? Well – I won't die, I guess. Say I start a business of my own, of some kind. Even if it doesn't work, I'm still young and able-bodied, and I still have marketable skills. I could still get a job. So – worst comes to worst – I'd be right back here, no worse off than I already am."

Fred leaned forward, propping his forearms on his thighs, and fitting his fingertips together. A bemused smile took over his face.

"Let's see, now. Almost any way I look at it, I wouldn't be taking that much of a risk. And even if I choose something that doesn't work out, I could still choose something else. It's not like I only get one shot."

"Very few decisions in life are truly irreversible, Fred."

Fred chuckled. "Yeah – that's kind of a profound truth, isn't it? Life is not a one-shot deal. You get a lot of turns at bat, if you're willing to get in the game. What do I really have to lose?"

"What, indeed?"

Fred leaned back, stretched out his legs, and folded his arms across his chest. He gazed into the water of the little pond.

"So what I've figured out is that my shyness, or my fear of mixing with people, wasn't the only thing holding me back. The shyness was covering up the fear of failing. Once I started interacting with people, I couldn't use that as an excuse for being unhappy. Now I have to face the fear of failure – or the fear of deciding."

Fred stroked his chin and nodded, to himself, as if he'd finally found what he'd been looking for.

"Okay – I'm gonna do it."

"Do what, Fred?"

"I'm going to go into business for myself. I've been cooking up a concept for a career, actually for some months now, but I was never ready to really take a swing at it. Now, I'm ready."

- Fred -

"You're ready?"

"Yep. It's all about health and fitness. I've always been fitness oriented and health conscious. I've studied it quite a bit, actually. I'd like to become a physical therapist, with a specialty in exercise physiology. That's something that kind of calls to me – helping people, using my know-how – using what I'm really interested in anyway."

"Is anything holding you back?"

"Well – not really. I can't do it all in one jump. I figure it'll take me about three years to really get there, but I can get started right away. I'll need to finish my degree, and I can choose a concentration in the health sciences. Then I'll have to get a credential for physical therapy – I'll have to look into all that. Meanwhile, I can get a job as a fitness trainer at one of the gyms in town. The pay is lousy, but I'll get to meet some babes. I'll have to sit down and map it all out, kind of a marching plan."

Fred felt different. He felt as if he'd become a new Fred over these past few

- Fred -

weeks.

"Maybe I've reached the frog-stage, at least," he mused. He glanced at the frog. The frog blinked.

"And the next stage?"

"The next stage is to wake up the handsome prince," he laughed. The idea seemed a bit comical, but no less appealing.

"I think I've just about lifted the curse. I can't say I've gotten rid of all my demons, but I don't feel like I'm immobilized any more. I can do this."

Fred was aware of a new energy in his body. It felt like some kind of vital force, which had been blocked and held back, was now released. He felt whole, centered, and strong. It was an unfamiliar feeling, but one he definitely liked.

He stood up, stretched, and tossed his jacket across his shoulder.

"Thanks, Mr. Frog. I think I'm on the way."

- Fred -

As he walked toward the entrance of the little park, he turned, and smiled —

Plip!

- Fred -

Chapter Seven.
Frank and the Frog, Part Three

"Professor Frog? Are you there?" Frank's voice was more cheerful, more energetic, than he'd ever known it to be. He was surprised at how up-beat he felt.

As he sat on the bench, he looked around the little park, expecting to spot the frog somewhere. He felt certain it was there, somewhere, knowing he had come.

"Well, I've got the solution," he said, his voice a mixture of relief and satisfaction, as he sat forward on the edge of the bench. He felt eager to explain it all to the frog, almost like a schoolboy, proudly presenting his work to his favorite teacher.

"You have the solution?"

There was the frog, sitting on the same

little flat rock he'd occupied when Frank had first seen him. Frank grinned, glad to see his little counselor again.

"Yep – it's pretty well worked out. It all fits. I'm making a big change, but I'm definitely jumping out of my frog pan."

"It's a big change?"

"You bet." Frank leaned back on the bench. He stretched, and laced his fingers together behind his head. "It's going to work."

"What about your business?"

"Amazingly, I found a buyer for the business. Our biggest competitor is going to acquire the operation, and fold it into their company. They'll take over the debt and even pay us a few bucks as well. We still have a good client list, we have a really good management staff, and we have a good software system that they want. So, we're worth more to them alive than dead, and it gets one of their competitors out of the market."

"And your partners?"

"My partners will do OK. Each of them

gets a payout – maybe not as much as they'd like, but they've had a pretty decent return on their money. I think they're pretty realistic about the situation."

"And your wife?"

"Well, the situation with Fran was less painful than I expected. We both agreed to an amicable divorce. She wants to start a new career, which means going back to school. By the time we sell the house and settle our bills, there's still a bit of dough for each of us. Enough for her to get a new start, and enough for me to do my thing."

"And what's your THING, Frank?"

"I got three job offers – it's amazing. All three are with international relief agencies. I'll have to go through a lot of training, and I'm not sure where I'll be assigned. But, I figure if I made it through Vietnam, I can take care of myself."

Frank rested his elbows on his knees, fitted his fingertips together, and ran through his mental checklist one more time.

"I've been doing a lot of research — Internet sites, country profiles, field manuals. I've been meeting some people who are doing that kind of work, and I'm learning a lot from them."

He glanced at the frog, with a satisfied smile. "You know, I can't believe how everything started falling into place, once I stopped fixating on my problems and started thinking more creatively — looking further for solutions. The things that sounded so far out don't seem so far out now, at all."

"Sometimes the solutions are hidden inside the problems."

Frank nodded, musing about the simple truth of that statement. "Yeah — I guess that's true."

Frank stood up, hitched up his pants, and put on his sunglasses. He turned to walk away, somewhat reluctantly. He stopped and turned, looking at the frog intently.

- Frank -

"I can't begin to tell you how grateful I am – how helpful these conversations have been. And how much this new insight means to me. I'll think about you, Mr. Frog. Maybe, somehow, I can talk to you again some time."

"I'll be here, Frank."

Plip!

Chapter Eight.
Fran and the Frog, Part Three

Fran was whistling a tune as she walked into the little park. She stopped to enjoy the secluded little place, its sounds and smells. It had become a special place for her. She felt more alive, more cheerful, more positive than she'd felt in a very long time.

"I've got some good news, Mr. Frog," she chirped. "Really good news."

"Good news?"

"Ah, there you are. I'd really be disappointed if I couldn't find you to share all of this with you."

"You seem very happy."

"Oh, I am," Fran said. She reached into her shoulder bag and pulled out an airline ticket, brandishing it with pride.

"I'm on my way. I enroll in the university two weeks from today – I'll be majoring in literature and writing. My eventual goal is to teach in a college somewhere. I got into the school I've always dreamed of, and I managed to get advanced placement. I'll start as a third-year student. It's gonna be great! I'm still a little scared, but ..."

"Scared of what?"

"Well ... I don't know – it's just that I don't have every little detail worked out. I'm so used to living every day by a fixed set of rules, that it just feels kind of funny making my own rules."

"Are there any unsolved problems?"

"Oh – nothing I can't handle, really. I still need to get a job, to pay my expenses. But I can do that, some way. I've waited on tables before, and I can do it again if I have to. Slinging hash for a while is a small price to pay for a whole new life. And, who knows? – maybe I can even get a job on campus as a teaching assistant."

- Fran -

"And your mother?"

"Well, that's the really amazing part of all this. I was kind of dreading the conversation with her, but it turned out pretty much like my mental movie – actually, far better."

"Better than your movie?"

"Yeah. I'd rehearsed it over and over in my mind, mostly concentrating on not feeling guilty or afraid. I pictured her as listening to me, and not going off on a tirade. When I told her what I wanted to do, she said she thought it was a great idea. She was genuinely happy that I was going to be able to make a career – something she'd never had. She even said she was proud of me."

"She reacted more positively than you expected?"

"It was amazing. We actually talked on a real, personal level – for the first time I can ever remember."

Fran chuckled. "It got real sappy, actually. We both cried, and I hugged her for the first time in ages. I told her I loved her and she told me she loved me, and that she was proud of me."

Tears were streaming down Fran's face. She sniffled and pulled a packet of disposable tissues out of her shoulder bag. She dabbed at her eyes. She sat quietly for a few moments.

"And your mother's health?"

"Well, that's another amazing thing. She actually brought up the idea of moving into a residential care home. She felt she needed to have closer medical supervision, and she'd actually been thinking about it for quite a while. Her pension will just about cover the costs. And, I'll just have to budget a little extra so I can fly back and visit her, maybe once a month or so. It's not really a problem."

"And your husband?"

"Well, that's all ironed out, too. I had a long talk with Frank, and we both agreed that we were going down two different roads. An amicable divorce seemed like the sensible thing to do. He sold his company and we settled up financially – he was very generous, under the circumstances. He has enough to start a whole new career, and I have enough to get mine started. We both did OK."

She paused and looked off into space, with a kind of a sweet smirk on her face.

"Funny …"

"What's funny?"

"That was the first really close conversation we'd had for a long, long time. He kissed me and told me he loved me – that he'd always love me."

Fran chuckled.

"One thing led to another, and I dragged him off to bed. We spent the whole afternoon."

She glanced at the frog. The frog looked away.

"Am I embarrassing you, Mr. Frog?"

The frog looked at Fran, and blinked. She laughed.

"Well, anyway, that's my story. A happy ending if ever I saw one."

- Fran -

"Or a happy beginning."

"A happy beginning? Yes! Yes, indeed. That's a much better way of saying it. It's like the end of one thing is the beginning of another thing."

"That sounds like my line."

She laughed, taken by surprise at the ironic remark. "Well, you do have a personality, after all."

Fran gazed into the water of the pond, reflecting on the changes in her life.

"I guess I can say the new movie is getting started. I don't know exactly how it's going to turn out, but at least it will be *my* movie."

Fran stood up, swung her shoulder bag across her shoulder, and turned to go. She lingered for a long moment, looking at the frog.

"I don't know how to thank you. You've given me a strength I never knew I had."

"You've always had it. Now you know you have it."

"Well, I'm going to miss you. I hope I can

find you again, sometime, somewhere.
Maybe I can tell you about my struggles
and my progress. I feel like you're a part
of me."

"I am, Fran."

Plip!

Chapter Nine.
Fred and the Frog, Part Three

Fred walked like a man with a mission. He unslung his backpack from his shoulder and sat down on the park bench, surveying the pond and the rocks around its edge.

"I've got some good news, Professor," he smiled, searching – hoping to see his frog-mentor.

"Good news?"

Fred started, pleased to see the frog perched on the lily pad. A second ago he couldn't see it. Now he could.

"There you are," he beamed. "Thanks for materializing." The frog blinked.

"I've got a plan, man. I know what I'm going to do."

- Fred -

"A plan?"

"Yup. I decided to pass up the default option and go for something instead of nothing. I'm going to make the career move. I can be a licensed physical therapist in about two years. I'm really jazzed about it. I start college today."

"And your job?"

"Well, I'll probably be making less money for a while. I've lined up a part-time job as a fitness trainer. And I have a couple of private clients I'm coaching."

"I told Frank – he's my boss – that I'm planning to change tracks, and he wished me well. He sold the company, so I'm not so sure I would have had a job for the long run anyway. He asked me if I'd stay on, part-time, to help with the transition. But he's a good guy, and I'm happy to help him out. He even arranged for me to get paid a bonus."

"So, you'll be going back to school?"

"Yeah. Actually, I only have a year and a half to do. Then I'll have my bachelor's degree. And I can take the courses for my physical therapy program at the same time. So, I just have to get along on reduced rations until I get all my tickets, and then I'll have a real career."

"Sounds like everything is worked out."

"Well, pretty much. I still have to work on the self-confidence, and I need to do more to mix with other people."

Fred smiled, looking off into space.

"There's another piece of good news, too."

"What's that?"

"I met a girl – a real nice girl. A woman, actually. I should stop calling them girls. They're women – and I'm a man."

It felt funny to Fred to refer to himself as a man. It was time to start.

"She's a nice person?"

"Yeah – she's really great. She's a nurse, so we have something in common. She's going to help me with my courses. We're not necessarily going steady or anything, but she's a lot of fun to be with."

Fred looked at the frog. The frog looked

at Fred.

"Do you have a girl friend, Mr. Frog?"

The frog blinked and looked away.

"Okay, okay, it's none of my business. You're my guiding spirit. I shouldn't be talking to you that way."

Fred stood up & stretched, feeling more relaxed and yet more focused than he could ever remember himself feeling. It felt great to know where he was going. "Well, I'd better get over to my first class," he said, slinging his backpack across his shoulder. "I'm a little rusty, but I figure I'll catch up pretty quick."

He paused, and turned. "Mr. Frog?"

"Yes, Fred?"

"I don't know who you are, or what you are, or anything about you, but I know one thing. You've helped me figure out who I am and what I want to become. I've still got a lot of growing to do. But I can't thank you enough for everything."

He smiled at the frog. The frog blinked.

"I hope I can talk to you again, maybe,

now and then. I'm not sure I feel a hundred percent like the prince yet, but I feel like that's where I'm heading. Will you still be my guide-frog?"

"Sure, Fred."

"Thanks."

Fred turned and walked toward the entrance of the little park.

"Fred?"

Fred stopped and turned. "Yes, sir?"

"Maybe you can be someone else's frog."

Fred paused and thought for a moment. He nodded.

"Hey – maybe I can. Yeah. Thanks."

He walked away, whistling softly.

Plip!

- Fred -

Made in the USA
Middletown, DE
07 June 2023

32197602R00064